This Book

BELONGS TO:

_____

IF LOST PLEASE:

 _____

✉ _____

TIME TABLE

SEMESTER:

START DATE: **END DATE:**

TIME	MON.	TUES.	WED.	THURS.	FRI.

TIME TABLE

SEMESTER:

START DATE: END DATE:

TIME	MON.	TUES.	WED.	THURS.	FRI.

TIME TABLE

SEMESTER:

START DATE: END DATE:

TIME	MON.	TUES.	WED.	THURS.	FRI.

Calendar

	S	M	T	W	T	F	S	
Month								WEEK 1
								WEEK 2
								WEEK 3
								WEEK 4
								WEEK 5

Assignments At a Glance

	MON	TUES	WED	THURS	FRI
WEEK 1					
WEEK 2					
WEEK 3					
WEEK 4					
WEEK 5					

ASSIGNMENTS - WEEK 1

MON	
TUES	
WED	
THURS	
FRI	

ASSIGNMENTS - WEEK 2

MON	
TUES	
WED	
THURS	
FRI	

ASSIGNMENTS - WEEK 3

MON	
TUES	
WED	
THURS	
FRI	

ASSIGNMENTS - WEEK 4

MON	
TUES	
WED	
THURS	
FRI	

ASSIGNMENTS - WEEK 5

MON	
TUES	
WED	
THURS	
FRI	

Calendar

	S	M	T	W	T	F	S	
Month								WEEK 1
								WEEK 2
								WEEK 3
								WEEK 4
								WEEK 5

Assignments At a Glance

	MON	TUES	WED	THURS	FRI
WEEK 1					
WEEK 2					
WEEK 3					
WEEK 4					
WEEK 5					

ASSIGNMENTS - WEEK 1

MON	
TUES	
WED	
THURS	
FRI	

ASSIGNMENTS - WEEK 2

MON	
TUES	
WED	
THURS	
FRI	

ASSIGNMENTS - WEEK 3

MON	
TUES	
WED	
THURS	
FRI	

ASSIGNMENTS - WEEK 4

MON	
TUES	
WED	
THURS	
FRI	

ASSIGNMENTS - WEEK 5

MON	
TUES	
WED	
THURS	
FRI	

Calendar

Month	S	M	T	W	T	F	S	
								WEEK 1
								WEEK 2
								WEEK 3
								WEEK 4
								WEEK 5

Assignments At a Glance

	MON	TUES	WED	THURS	FRI
WEEK 1					
WEEK 2					
WEEK 3					
WEEK 4					
WEEK 5					

ASSIGNMENTS - WEEK 1

MON	
TUES	
WED	
THURS	
FRI	

ASSIGNMENTS - WEEK 2

MON	
TUES	
WED	
THURS	
FRI	

ASSIGNMENTS - WEEK 3

MON	
TUES	
WED	
THURS	
FRI	

ASSIGNMENTS - WEEK 4

MON	
TUES	
WED	
THURS	
FRI	

ASSIGNMENTS - WEEK 5

MON	
TUES	
WED	
THURS	
FRI	

Calendar

Month	S	M	T	W	T	F	S	
								WEEK 1
								WEEK 2
								WEEK 3
								WEEK 4
								WEEK 5

Assignments At a Glance

	MON	TUES	WED	THURS	FRI
WEEK 1					
WEEK 2					
WEEK 3					
WEEK 4					
WEEK 5					

ASSIGNMENTS - WEEK 1

MON	
TUES	
WED	
THURS	
FRI	

ASSIGNMENTS - WEEK 2

MON	
TUES	
WED	
THURS	
FRI	

ASSIGNMENTS - WEEK 3

MON	
TUES	
WED	
THURS	
FRI	

ASSIGNMENTS - WEEK 4

MON	
TUES	
WED	
THURS	
FRI	

ASSIGNMENTS - WEEK 5

MON	
TUES	
WED	
THURS	
FRI	

Calendar

	S	M	T	W	T	F	S	
Month								WEEK 1
								WEEK 2
								WEEK 3
								WEEK 4
								WEEK 5

Assignments At a Glance

	MON	TUES	WED	THURS	FRI
WEEK 1					
WEEK 2					
WEEK 3					
WEEK 4					
WEEK 5					

ASSIGNMENTS - WEEK 1

MON	
TUES	
WED	
THURS	
FRI	

ASSIGNMENTS - WEEK 2

MON	
TUES	
WED	
THURS	
FRI	

ASSIGNMENTS - WEEK 3

MON	
TUES	
WED	
THURS	
FRI	

ASSIGNMENTS - WEEK 4

MON	
TUES	
WED	
THURS	
FRI	

ASSIGNMENTS - WEEK 5

MON	
TUES	
WED	
THURS	
FRI	

Calendar

Month	S	M	T	W	T	F	S	
								WEEK 1
								WEEK 2
								WEEK 3
								WEEK 4
								WEEK 5

Assignments At a Glance

	MON	TUES	WED	THURS	FRI
WEEK 1					
WEEK 2					
WEEK 3					
WEEK 4					
WEEK 5					

ASSIGNMENTS - WEEK 1

MON	
THU	
WED	
THURS	
FRI	

ASSIGNMENTS - WEEK 2

MON	
TUES	
WED	
THURS	
FRI	

ASSIGNMENTS - WEEK 3

MON	
TUES	
WED	
THURS	
FRI	

ASSIGNMENTS - WEEK 4

MON	
TUES	
WED	
THURS	
FRI	

ASSIGNMENTS - WEEK 5

MON

TUES

WED

THURS

FRI

Calendar

	S	M	T	W	T	F	S	
Month								WEEK 1
								WEEK 2
								WEEK 3
								WEEK 4
								WEEK 5

Assignments At a Glance

	MON	TUES	WED	THURS	FRI
WEEK 1					
WEEK 2					
WEEK 3					
WEEK 4					
WEEK 5					

ASSIGNMENTS - WEEK 1

MON	
TUES	
WED	
THURS	
FRI	

ASSIGNMENTS - WEEK 2

MON	
TUES	
WED	
THURS	
FRI	

ASSIGNMENTS - WEEK 3

MON	
TUES	
WED	
THURS	
FRI	

ASSIGNMENTS - WEEK 4

MON	
TUES	
WED	
THURS	
FRI	

ASSIGNMENTS - WEEK 5

MON	
TUES	
WED	
THURS	
FRI	

Calendar

	s	M	T	W	T	F	S	
Month								WEEK 1
								WEEK 2
								WEEK 3
								WEEK 4
								WEEK 5

Assignments At a Glance

	MON	TUES	WED	THURS	FRI
WEEK 1					
WEEK 2					
WEEK 3					
WEEK 4					
WEEK 5					

ASSIGNMENTS - WEEK 1

MON	
TUES	
WED	
THURS	
FRI	

ASSIGNMENTS - WEEK 2

MON

TUES

WED

THURS

FRI

ASSIGNMENTS - WEEK 3

MON	
TUES	
WED	
THURS	
FRI	

ASSIGNMENTS - WEEK 4

MON	
TUES	
WED	
THURS	
FRI	

ASSIGNMENTS - WEEK 5

MON	
TUES	
WED	
THURS	
FRI	

Calendar

Month	S	M	T	W	T	F	S	
								WEEK 1
								WEEK 2
								WEEK 3
								WEEK 4
								WEEK 5

Assignments At a Glance

	MON	TUES	WED	THURS	FRI
WEEK 1					
WEEK 2					
WEEK 3					
WEEK 4					
WEEK 5					

ASSIGNMENTS - WEEK 1

MON	
TUES	
WED	
THURS	
FRI	

ASSIGNMENTS - WEEK 2

MON	
TUES	
WED	
THURS	
FRI	

ASSIGNMENTS - WEEK 3

MON	
TUES	
WED	
THURS	
FRI	

ASSIGNMENTS - WEEK 4

MON	
TUES	
WED	
THURS	
FRI	

ASSIGNMENTS - WEEK 5

MON	
TUES	
WED	
THURS	
FRI	

Calendar

	S	M	T	W	T	F	S	
Month								WEEK 1
								WEEK 2
								WEEK 3
								WEEK 4
								WEEK 5

Assignments At a Glance

	MON	TUES	WED	THURS	FRI
WEEK 1					
WEEK 2					
WEEK 3					
WEEK 4					
WEEK 5					

ASSIGNMENTS - WEEK 1

MON	
TUES	
WED	
THURS	
FRI	

ASSIGNMENTS - WEEK 2

MON	
TUES	
WED	
THURS	
FRI	

ASSIGNMENTS - WEEK 3

MON	
TUES	
WED	
THURS	
FRI	

ASSIGNMENTS - WEEK 4

MON	
TUES	
WED	
THURS	
FRI	

ASSIGNMENTS - WEEK 5

MON	
TUES	
WED	
THURS	
FRI	

Calendar

Month	S	M	T	W	T	F	S	
								WEEK 1
								WEEK 2
								WEEK 3
								WEEK 4
								WEEK 5

Assignments At a Glance

	MON	TUES	WED	THURS	FRI
WEEK 1					
WEEK 2					
WEEK 3					
WEEK 4					
WEEK 5					

ASSIGNMENTS - WEEK 1

MON	
TUES	
WED	
THURS	
FRI	

ASSIGNMENTS - WEEK 2

MON	
TUES	
WED	
THURS	
FRI	

ASSIGNMENTS - WEEK 3

MON	
TUES	
WED	
THURS	
FRI	

ASSIGNMENTS - WEEK 4

MON	
TUES	
WED	
THURS	
FRI	

ASSIGNMENTS - WEEK 5

MON	
TUES	
WED	
THURS	
FRI	

Calendar

Month	S	M	T	W	T	F	S	
								WEEK 1
								WEEK 2
								WEEK 3
								WEEK 4
								WEEK 5

Assignments At a Glance

	MON	TUES	WED	THURS	FRI
WEEK 1					
WEEK 2					
WEEK 3					
WEEK 4					
WEEK 5					

ASSIGNMENTS - WEEK 1

MON	
TUES	
WED	
THURS	
FRI	

ASSIGNMENTS - WEEK 2

MON	
TUES	
WED	
THURS	
FRI	

ASSIGNMENTS - WEEK 3

MON	
TUES	
WED	
THURS	
FRI	

ASSIGNMENTS - WEEK 4

MON	
TUES	
WED	
THURS	
FRI	

ASSIGNMENTS - WEEK 5

MON	
TUES	
WED	
THURS	
FRI	

weight
(rounded to the nearest whole number)

IMPERIAL	METRIC
0.5 oz	14 g
1 oz	28 g
2 oz	58 g
3 oz	86 g
4 oz	114 g
5 oz	142 g
6 oz	170 g
7 oz	198 g
8 oz (1/2 lb)	226 g
9 oz	256 g
10 oz	284 g
11 oz	312 g
12 oz	340 g
13 oz	368 g
14 oz	396 g
15 oz	426 g
16 oz (1 lb)	454 g
24 oz (1 1/2 lb)	680 g

misc
(rounded to the closest equivalent)

IMPERIAL	
1 quart	4 cups (1 liter)
4 quarts	16 cups (4.5 liters)
6 quarts	24 cups (7 liters)
1 gallon	16 cups (4.5 liters)

volume
(rounded to the closest equivalent)

IMPERIAL	METRIC
1/8 tsp	0.5 mL
1/4 tsp	1 mL
1/2 tsp	2.5 mL
3/4 tsp	4 mL
1 tsp	5 mL
1 tbsp	15 mL
1 1/2 tbsp	25 mL
1/8 cup	30 mL
1/4 cup	60 mL
1/3 cup	80 mL
1/2 cup	120 mL
2/3 cup	160 mL
3/4 cup	180 mL
1 cup	240 mL

liquid
(rounded to the closest equivalent)

IMPERIAL	METRIC
0.5 oz	15 mL
1 oz	30 mL
2 oz	60 mL
3 oz	85 mL
4 oz	115 mL
5 oz	140 mL
6 oz	170 mL
7 oz	200 mL
8 oz	230 mL
9 oz	260 mL
10 oz	285 mL
11 oz	310 mL
12 oz	340 mL
13 oz	370 mL

temperature
(rounded to the closest equivalent)

IMPERIAL	METRIC
150°F	65°C
160 °F	70 °C
175 °F	80 °C
200 °F	95 °C
225 °F	110 °C
250 °F	120 °C
275 °F	135 °C
300 °F	150 °C
325 °F	160 °C
350 °F	175 °C
375 °F	190 °C
400 °F	205 °C
425 °F	220 °C
450 °F	230 °C
475 °F	245 °C
500 °F	260 °C

length
(rounded to the closest equivalent)

IMPERIAL	METRIC
1/8 inch	3 mm
1/4 inch	6 mm
1 inch	2.5 cm
1 1/4 inch	3 cm
2 inches	5 cm
6 inches	15 cm
8 inches	20 cm
9 inches	22.5 cm
10 inches	25 cm
11 inches	28 cm